MAKING LANDFALL

MAKING LANDFALL

Paul Lindholdt

Encircle Publications, LLC
Farmington, Maine USA

Making Landfall Copyright ©2018 Paul Lindholdt
Paperback ISBN-13: 978-1-948338-50-9
e-Book ISBN 13: 978-1-948338-51-6

All rights reserved. No part of this book may be reproduced in any form by any mechanical or electronic means including storage and retrieval systems without express written permission in writing from the publisher. Brief passages may be quoted in review.

Editor: Cynthia Brackett-Vincent
Book and book cover design: Eddie Vincent/ENC Graphics Services
Cover Images: Map—Shutterstock;
Painting—"The Landing of the Pilgrims" by Michel Felice Corné," used with permission Pilgrim Hall Museum

Author photograph: Karen Lindholdt

Printing: Walch Publishing, Portland, Maine

Mail Orders, Author Inquiries:
Encircle Publications
PO Box 187
Farmington, ME 04938
207-778-0467

Online orders:
http://encirclepub.com

ACKNOWLEDGEMENTS

My foremost thanks go to my writing mentor Annie Dillard, who ignited flames of inspiration within me. My late PhD adviser, Harrison Meserole, taught me the ropes and rewards of research in early American culture. Friends who kindly read and improved this book in manuscript include Polly Buckingham, Dan Butterworth, and Leona Vander Molen. The Northwest Institute for Advanced Study awarded me a gift of time to finish the project.

Some of these poems have appeared in the following books and periodicals and been revised since their first appearance:

Antigonish Review, "The Plumed Clod"

Beloit Poetry Journal, "Brood Slave"

Blessing the Animals, "Song of Salmon"

Chicago Review, "Rebecca Glover," "Another Wild," and "Here and Now"

Common-place, "Triptych" (now "Gorgeana Escorts"), "Sarah Hawkridge," "The Great Awakening" and "Mary Dyer"

Fugue, "Cotton Mather" (now "Cotton Mather, Exorcist"), "Marianne's Quarters," and "The Glare of Her Awareness"

Jeopardy, "Warbler"

Poet Lore, "Cattail" and "Barnyard Artist"

Poetry Northwest, "Crossing Arbon Valley," "Yeoman" (now "Moll Gone"), and "Malad"

Railtown Almanac, "Brooding Season"

Sewanee Review, "Traveler to the Colonies," "Promoter of the Colonies," "Kit Gardiner, Banished," and "Inscription" (now "Epitaph").

Slackwater Review, "The Horse"

Southern Humanities Review, "Magistrate" and "Ouzel"

TABLE OF CONTENTS

Acknowledgments

Brooding Season

Traveler to the Colonies	3
The Gorgeana Escorts	5
Brooding Season	7
Song of Salmon	8
King Philip	9
How the Powwow Found Her	10
Thomas Morton	11
Famacides	13
The Plumed Clod	15
Promoter of the Colonies	17

Line of Descent

Sarah Hawkridge	20
Another Wild	21
Homage to Mistress Bradford	23
The Sleeper	24
Here and Now	25
Rebecca Glover	26
Governor Winthrop	28
Mary Dyer	29
Landfall	30

Flowers Washed in Our Wake

Tenochtitlan	32
Cattail	34
Ouzel	35
Warbler	36
The Horse	37
Crossing Arbon Valley	38
Moll Gone	40
The Glare of Her Awareness	42
The Banquet of Saint Anthony	43

When Land Grows Fat

Kit Gardiner, Banished	48
Buck Meadows	50
Benediction	51
Anniversary	52
Magistrate	53
Marianne's Quarters	55
Grain on the Fields	57
Malad	59

Merchant Saints

John Winter to Moses Goodyear	62
Cotton Mather, Exorcist	63

The Great Swamp Fight from the Pulpit Construed	64
The Hawthorn Tree	66
Barnyard Artist	68
Brood Slave	70
Arrowhead Hunting at Kinport Peak	72
The Great Awakening	73
Epitaph	74
Notes	75
About the Author	81

BROODING SEASON

*"Outside the New World winters in grand dark
white air lashing high thro' the virgin stands
foxes down foxholes sigh,
surely the English heart quails, stunned."*

— John Berryman

TRAVELER TO THE COLONIES

It was like being forced to live
a new death each fifth breath—
that sliding of the ship up troughs
three times its height, that slamming
back to hear each timber groan.
Waves ramped high to challenge heaven;
heaven to sea descended.
No light shone, till in a blaze
sea and ship were galvanized by flame
and twitched before they froze.
Our mizzen shroud lines flapping,
the stern mast cracked and fell
across the capstan until the master
pressed a mate to hack it free.
Three weeks from Gravesend we wallowed,
bound out for Pascataway in Maine.

Commenced the same way all harm starts:
lure of marvels, riches, land
beyond all kenning. One might pluck fowls
from low-hung limb, or skewer up
bass on spits beside the bay.
Red stags frisked and fed from hand.
Gold, the Spaniard's bliss,
oozed down stone out liquid seams.
And the sea, its face lay always
calm and fair, its breath restorative
and sweet. Saucers of marrow
found in cods' heads cured black moods.
Fish of all kinds leapt to net.
So it seemed from what we read.
So this place seemed
from what the sly promoters said.

Instead we sleep in canvas shacks
hemmed close by ruts of mud
frozen. We hear the wilderness all night
howling for our souls. Indians send
their black god Abbamocho
to us. We saw him fly past one dusk,
rope dangling between his legs.
He makes the muffled moon to whine
at our doorstep, shore stones
gnash and grind. *Join us, pawn your wit
and join us*, the darkness cries.
Witches also there be many,
spider-bellied witches, if you believe report,
and thornback monsters born
to those outside the fold. We eat
salted hake and groundnuts dug from dirt.

How many travelers before me have you
enticed from cozy fireside to try
your surface, flattering sea?
In a restful harbor, a glazed bay,
I have sworn you hold more heaven
than sky itself is freighted by.
Turn aside your wimpled wave, now, go.
No more beyond this voyage will I stir
to mingle my fate with yours.
Expect no further love from me.
I shall build a cedar cabin
at Hell's Gate and rest there
cloistered from your strumpet ways.
I shall write the truth about this land
and warn my countrymen to guard their eyes.

THE GORGEANA ESCORTS

Thomas Wannerton

Too cumbersome, my musket, no matter how
wolves skulked about the sheep pens after dark.
So I refused to carry it on my hikes.
For my rashness Tom scolded me and downed
a pint of kill-devil rum in one fast draught
to charm away all harm. My herbal served
me better out of doors—that fat folio book
by Gerard kept the gathered leaves pressed fresh.
One late evening when I got home, Tom drank
and slept in fits. At midnight he rose up
shouting: wolves as dense as Hannibal's troops
were sieging the house, he cried, chasing sheep.
From his voice one ram fled, lunged at a fence,
thrashed and bawled there, impaled on whetted stake.

Richard Foxwell

His sharp and upright ears held no round folds.
The cabin candle daubed them oxblood red.
Tongues of smoke lolled out of his pipe and curled
up his cheeks, as if they would lick his whiskers.
He stirred sugar in his Port and told how
to understand this new world by its omens.
Listen outside town when the moon is down,
the wind exhausted after blowing. There
a sweet voice called out to him, *Foxwell, Foxwell,
test your wings*. And in the clouds a fire shone
where folks frisked naked in a ring. He would
dance with them, wear his hair in tufts like theirs
and mince burn-free in the flames, did he not
love the comforts of pipe and cup so much.

Michael Mitton

Reeds and the beech trees leaning, sea gusts
trumpeting across the cove, geese rose
off the water yelping then crumpled
before we heard his gun thud.
He swung the wounded birds like plumb bobs.
Neatly afterward in his log he wrote
the lot, the charge, the wind-drift, shot and distance
alongside what fees the meat might fetch
in Boston. A great shot, a nonpareil, his eye
can out a fowl's at three rods, and yet
his hands curl just like mine in every way.
The housewives who buy his wares
bend to their task on the beach and send
the plucked down lofting across the waves.

BROODING SEASON

Farther and farther the partridge fled
peeping, feigning a hurt wing, luring the dog
away from its hidden nest at field's edge,
landing on the weedy turf only long
enough to give the spaniel hope, open-mouthed,
bounding and reckless of our commands.
We'd come in June, brooding season, eggs
still hatching, chicks unfledged,
wrong to have brought Silky-Coat trained
for the chase, lost in the capture and kill.

If we were Puritans bound to morality tales
we might say she loses herself to instinct every day
while we mislay ourselves only in the fall.
But we were living closely in the moment,
hooting for the partridge to escape
and dupe the dog, that hunter accustomed to
dozing at our feet, and our best philosophies
could subtract no tension from the scene
or sketch it in ethical shades. From the field
we minded a partridge wing up and out of sight.

SONG OF SALMON

Translated from the Kwak'wala

Many are running into shore,
others with me,
true salmon gone the long way.

They are running into shore
to you: stout pole
at the center of the heavens.

Dancing from the far world to shore
with me now,
true salmon gone the long way,

know that they run dancing
to you: right side
of the face of the heavens.

Towering beyond, and reaching past,
and outshining all,
true salmon gone the long way.

KING PHILIP

These furs and wampum strings are mine.
I trapped the mink and drilled the shells.
But when friends bury my corpse upright
nothing will adorn these slack breasts

I leave to my sons. I will drive
away the English forever then.
From their bubbling crocks of wine
I'll take stain. From the smallpox, stench.

Among the piles of skulls that hide
beside stones, I will rise to wreck
fence and blast rye field. The wild eye
the whites brought oversea grows red

among them yet. They fear the tongues
of daughters who oppose their laws
and sermons, their judgments and guns.
Witches those women will be called

and dandled by their necks till quiet.
Why do Bostons bring so much dread?
May the wheels of their carts collide
and ship masts crack before my breath.

HOW THE POWWOW FOUND HER

Toddling

lost in the woods
kicked in the head
torn like a loaf
dragged from the bed

born in a field
thrashed in a shed
dropped from a cliff
mistaken for dead

Brain-Struck

I trace the Boston fever to its source—
a sick soul my throbbing drums
drive back to the other side.

I thump and grunt, hunch and scowl
until the sickly liquor at last
bleeds through her thin ear-sheath.

Feral

Someone invited her and she came late.
Bowing and rasping in heron plumes,
rubbing rat-fur cuffs, sulfur
smeared on her face and chest,
she crouched silent, sober, watchful
till her groaning yelps disrupted the nuptials.

THOMAS MORTON

I never sold the natives rum or Madeira
wine; I gave it to them as friends.
Around the crock we capered
and howled alongside the old hound
when the tide of Portuguese wine
rose in our guts belt-high.

You might have liked to frisk with us
around the antlered maypole,
Mister Endecott. Instead
you chopped it down and burnt our huts.
If I were counsel, I'd have you flailed
while friends grilled gobbets of your horse.

Out in the square, past the bars of my cell,
you drill troops and swell for war.
You pass and I hiss there's no need,
the natives already are dropping
from the pox, but my voice sounds
as faint as theirs and your shouts drum.

Out on a porch you gagged a scold
and propped her up in stocks for all to see.
She'll remember you in prayer.
So will John Crowse
whose tongue, because he swore,
you had a hole bored with a red-hot rod.

Each evening at Moorfield the curfew bell
demands stray walkers
close themselves behind doors.
Amid such silence, illness twists my belly
and my feverish pulse
roars like a storm in both hot ears.

Snowmelt trickling down a root hair
quickens worms to stir
beneath shelves of stone.
Maybe I won't know when the pox
contracts to advocate for me.

FAMACIDES

In early spring I came
to his cabin's remains, saw birch limbs
hanging black against low clouds.
Brought along his dog
the neighbors found ax-whipped
and left to die in the wood,
hound now blind in the right eye.
It snuffed and yelped
as the hopeful home smells multiplied.

Horace or Herodotus, I forget which,
had a name for those who smear
the names of gentle women and men—
famacides. To murder character,
to blotch good fame, has come to be so
common now. Pencils and pens
like twelve-pound mauls.
Anecdotes like inkpots flung.
Father's father never sold
the Indians rum or muskets as was claimed.

Timbers scorched from ceiling to floor,
one wall fallen away from the frame,
dark logs darker from panicked fir-pitch
seeping. The hurt hound
whined to fly away to wholesome air,
to burdock, woundwort,
sassafras and brome grass.

Beneath a hawthorn tree overlooking the sea
my grandsire long ago had buried
a lead urn holding gold.
I knelt and dug it up. From its mouth
coins spilled out upon the ground.

Gold that shone like the teeth
of a nobleman so fever-shot
I knew my lobelia poultice was too late.

THE PLUMED CLOD

From a swallow nest now crumbling,
    from its mud shell lined with grass,
feathers, horsehair; the mud
    first mixed with saliva, borne

by mouthfuls, spat into place,
    extruded—the nest I dashed
to the dooryard beside wasp hives
    and mouse droppings—from it falls

something dried and dense
    like dung but gaudy, oddly
plumed I see as I lift it to the light.
    Grey, oblong, its one inch

tapers to a fine point where a white
    feather protrudes, like the hooded
cilia of a barnacle feeding at sea.
    Where the base of fine plume

disappears, a beak clamped
    on the shaft of the plume emerges
above a string of tiny spinal knobs.
    That is when I recognize

the hatchling's legs that clench and curl
    like hairs. Superstition intrudes
and I yearn to be rid of it, shut the dry
    corpse out of sight, carry it far away

from the cabin, but something in its small life
    invites me to merge it with mine
and envision how it had been. The blind
    mouth groping toward shadow, nourished

by the arrival of shade, feeding and clacking
    when light paused and stuffed it,
then swallowing the bit of nest
    halfway till breathing ceased and hunger

also fled. This must be the way faint songs
    subside. In my palm now it is
a plumed clod—weightless, insensible,
    a pinch away from brittle dust.

Outside, swallows skim the fir trees
    and flutter near the cabin
to start to build new nests. I need to sweep
    the eaves, brush away old webs

and return indoors to my lap desk
    and the clutter that erupts beside it.
The papers and other alien objects:
    a pewter pot, clay pipe, several books.

PROMOTER OF THE COLONIES

What would you say if you were to see
fields of clover knee-high

and bee-drowsy, ceaselessly flowering?
Fertile valleys crowded

with spruce trees beneath whose shade
you may stroll for days? Or turnips,

sown three weeks earlier, grown
large now as any a blacksmith's arm?

Pigeons crowd the sky for miles
and weave nest to nest, branch to branch

in marvels of twig architecture.
Bull moose, oxen of the woodlands, rear

twice man-height above the spongy loam
they tramp. This is the new world,

loaves and fishes, a granary laid out for those
ground down by hunger and hard luck.

LINE OF DESCENT

*"I was pirouette and flourish,
I was filigree and flame.
How could I count my blessings
when I didn't know their names?"*

—Rita Dove

SARAH HAWKRIDGE

Shy as a titmouse, my breath rose
each night your hand
lifted the latch.
Six children, Mister Cotton,
six rings of birth-fire for your name.

The gift of vision, the gospel speech,
did it descend upon you
unaware? You heard my poems
only rarely, when I dared.

At bedtime I settled on you
like a wreath.
The walls sustained
our silent straining each to each.

Husband, father, flail of faith,
you plucked my hem
last night from your deathbed.
And I could not sway you
from your fancy, could not pray,
you clung to me so.

ANOTHER WILD

Again it is snowing, more soups and stews.
This hearthstone and sizzling oak log
should suffice, but the finer things
in life beguile me—silk lace, rhymed verses,
cherry and plum marmalade.
Deer in the orchard rise to nibble frozen fruit.

The governor is studying alone.
He says we must feed upon the Word.
The kidskin vellum of his gilt-edged books,
ever-tender to the touch, binds up all
we know of earth and all we need to know.

He joins me nightly, flourishes me! For I am
his barren bride. That's why the congregation sighs
when we proceed down aisle to our pew.

Behind a desk the deacons sit, moneybox extended.
The poor drop in coins and see me twitch.
My legs quake, arms pimple, my neck bends.
I know how one king served his Catherine Howard.
Beneath the left breast—help me—a mole

begins to wax in my damp and shade.
The maid Kathleen would burn it off so no judge
summons me for grooming a third teat.
Whom shall I suckle? My belly
does not extend. Deer fold forelegs,
as if praying, when they reach up to feed.

Now he who claims to know me most
is muttering in study, husband
mouthing Ecclesiastes from the Hebrew.
Or maybe he is cursing my womb, hoping

to spit me, a doe above the firepit,
apple clenched at the last between her teeth.

HOMAGE TO MISTRESS BRADFORD

Out your home's back door I scuttle ash
and trim the plantain where you pace
the creek path. You lower your eyes
when you pass, never make a sound.
You are listening for the noise of joy.

Your worry comes in feathered waves
as if a bird were in your throat.
And I picture you lisping on a limb
beside the creek, the song of flight
beneath your bodice buttons
forbidden by every dictate of your place.

And I know you fear him and that is why
you study your feet. And I hear your
breath catch whenever he calls your name.
And I wait daylong for magic words
to rise to your lips, for you to behold me
as more than indentured servant, as a man.

Lift your eyes one time if you would fly.
Then step into the birch grove where
I am abiding to remind you who you are.

THE SLEEPER

Fallen asleep after supper,
wakened by the cat
at dusk, you saw stars
wetly daubed
above the treetop,
watched each one
begin to glint and fatten
past the cabin door.
But you whispered
"Morning," said it
over and over until
I woke you fully
that evening, I did, me.

HERE AND NOW

"I smell the cooking fire outside.
My nose is good another day!"
—Cree prayer

The hymnbook slips from my fingers.

My adult children across the aisle
shoot savage glances at me but too late.
Some inner spirit stirs
and already I am entering a wood
where Jeremiah's sermon can't follow.

I step through a wall of sumac
and the sudden autumn bush explodes
in grouse wings. My heart
reels beside them through the leaves.

Feathers and fruit fall, blaze
and decay, none of these may alarm me
when the smell of leaf mold
heavens my senses
and wing-beats blunt the pain of age.

REBECCA GLOVER

Almost gouged out both wide eyes
in a berry patch, Mason did,
the day he heard me
singing "Owyhee" by the spring.
He thrashed among briars, I combed my hair.
Owyhee! I still call like Mama.
Sip-sip-sip owyhoo. Pleasant nonsense
crooned to Bermuda slave tunes.
An easy way to add up all she said.

In the church she said I'd gain bad fame.
I wish I'd heeded her and hushed.
My loose hair, she warned me,
my azure brooch from southern seas.
Mason swore it winked
like a third eye, called my song
a dark curse cast to beguile the vines
that lashed and scratched him.
How otherwise did his house catch fire?

Before the flames from his manor died
the magistrate was charging me
as a witch. I bent head,
surrendered the brooch into his hands.
He consigned me to the bailiff
while I waited to be tried.
Owyhoo, I sung from a prison straw cot.
Weary with fear, I sung out.

Pictures crawled the walls all night.
Mistress Fray lashed to a stool
and plunged in a pond
while men leered. Anna Breen
forced to walk past a corpse

and see if its eyes opened at her sight.
I was informed I bore
Master Brown ill will.

He never lied, they said, never
seized Mother's acres when she died.

Kiss me now, Mason Brown.
Into your mouth
I'll puff a divine red wind
till you float among the stars.
And if I get my wish
on the third day you will rise again from life.

Kiss me now and taste the breeding
yeast I've fed on
to leaven these heavy hours.

GOVERNOR WINTHROP

In the course of the trial
to show the judge
how far she'd fallen, I ordered it

disinterred, her stillborn child.
Only that way could everyone see
the thornback monster she had whelped.

And it pleased God
to have kept the corpse from
putrefying all those eighteen weeks.

Strong men grimaced and the midwife
swooned again over the moon
eye, the thorn-ridged

spine, the talons
clenched where feet should be.
Those are the accessories heretics wear.

MARY DYER

Whoever comes to see my stillborn girl
might flinch to find my face
within the crowd. But there I'll crane
and press with the rest
as if the public stir concerned an inner light
flashed from some saint's eyes.

Winthrop ordered her displayed
to ripen the fruit of my desperate mood.

Unearthed with spades to gratify another round
of guests, she calls me now to rise
from mattress and join her
at the gravesite—still agitated that scales
veil each eye, that each ear hears
a summons to witness the error of my ways.

If they tell the truth who say a corpse will bleed
when viewed by the one who's slain,
let Winthrop come and watch the fresh beads well.
He'll call it magic when her wounds
gape wide again like mouths to spill his guilt.

LANDFALL

Daughter, it's the landfall of my voyage
that will bring me back to you.
The best reprieve after weeks at sea

still doesn't come, and won't show
and withholds from us the scent of soil,
the sight of shorebirds, oak leaves

afloat on swells. For you, sweetness,
I hired a sailor to clamber up
the mainmast after dark and lay his hands on

a falcon settled there to rest. I shall feed her
on boiled eggs and salt pork.
I shall stitch an Afghan hood from serge.

By the time you are a woman grown, she will
be flying for you, my Louisa, if
you choose to tame a creature of the wind.

Yourself and hawk and bonnet strings
partaking in the sport of kings
may make the lowly ground birds cower.

FLOWERS WASHED IN OUR WAKE

"So wickedness being here more stopped by strict laws...
it searches everywhere and at last breaks out where it gets vent."

—William Bradford

TENOCHTITLAN

They refused to yield
or even cease feeding when
we rode up and commanded their camp.
Not one flinched when I
drew my sword from
atop my horse—the same way
Gutierrez fluttered tribes
in Virginia to seize their pearls.
But my blade could sing
nothing. One turned a corn cake

on the fire. My children, I shall
overcome your trust.
I watched myself dismount, stoop
and behold their faces
as if I were praying my weakness
might rise no farther than my bent knees.
Maybe I did lisp a little plea.
The Lamb of God
delivers no fame
to soldiers cowed by heathen faith.

Beyond their eyes, Mexica Vieja
was already spinning
toward night like a tornado.
And from the hustling dust
their skeletons came
to rest beside the cooking pit.
So much at ease now
that lizards colonized the ribs
and snake heads watched from each jaw.
Valió la pena. It was worth the pain.

The roofs of Tenochtitlan
shone gold on the plain
as never before.
At that moment, a vision:
their aviaries leapt with flames
I would set. The souls inside—the tender
warblers, sparrows, wrens—
thrust beaks against the mesh
and uttered
cries keen enough to shave me.

CATTAIL

Sharp thin leaves
divined this desert isle,
its sere speck of shoreline.
Even as unsprung seeds
dung- and mud-bedded
between swallows' toes.
The wind, the alkali
and dust, suck moisture from
these cross-hatched leaves,
turning burlap the galled leaf's edge.

This stalk a fount,
an upright reservoir,
cornerstone for redwings.
Reed mace wielded when gods fought.
Strong stalk, pliant.
But will the soil provide?
Will the black stone crumble to grains
before my probing foot?
This is the desert pond my leaves
divined, this the shore.

OUZEL

*"The earth hath bubbles as the water has,
And these are of them."*
—Shakespeare

Among pebbles of the streambed
it dips and prods
now underwater, wings outstretched
for balance against the flow,
turning over stones
where small insects hide,
darting after them, clutching the bottom
as though on a vertical slide,
swept back then climbing
forward again, a liquid shuttle
grooming the streambed,
loosening debris that swirls
into the current, still underwater,
still prying, a squat
gray genius of balance,
voiceless and single-minded,
perpetually hungry,
never stepping twice
on the same stone, dipping
to seize larva, always
bobbing and searching
for food in the flux
of its home, the current
sliding past thin, clear
and insistent, the beak probing
between toes, wings clinging,
now breaking the surface to alight
on a trembling spruce branch
to rest and drip the wings.

WARBLER

Unaccountably the air congeals
in a space between trees
where people feed:
the earth rears cockeyed
and mountains slam.

Clamor, sunshafts,
these throb and dissolve
until the beak
dabbed in water
wakes and jabs the heavy hand.

What sounds abound like threats
above the head as if
to challenge the summer storm?
Captive heart, what harm
is sure to occur?

THE HORSE

The horse lies shouldered to earth
    by pain so slow to mount
that tansy weed might be to blame
    except none grows where the wind

now bends his vision. Whitened blades
    rattle and starve the face
for some moments. Where green spring
    fields used to grow, an illness

multiplies and divides. The broad ribs
    do not heave, nor the nostrils
pump to suck in air, but stiff ripples clip
    the spine from mane to rump

and drive the gelding flesh to flinch
    as though flyblown. The tail
furrows the sand before towering
    and falling to slap up a last dust bath.

CROSSING ARBON VALLEY

1.
Geography of thought forsaken by imagination
in this valley the bluestem yields to rue.
No one stirring, no soul at work
to discover Providence, stingy
as it is and sparse, nibbled
by crickets the sparrow hawks can't check.

Jawbone of an elk calf, teeth intact.
Grouse chick peeping beside Trickle Creek.
No men, no women, far as the eye…

2.
Ancestors fraught by modesty shunned
the word *I* in journals and logs.
Nephi drew the reins taut. Or: The minister
inveighed against Diantha's spruce lute.

Stiff gusts whistle across a lip of cliff,
dust devils scour smooth
the fading trail. First-person speech
still rare for humility's sake.

Spirit gulls peal, tugged by wires!

3.
But it's only a trick, trompe l'oeil,
these saints no more exempt
than Shakers or Anabaptist shepherds.

The lone tree, a locust, wears grooves
where a mutton puncher swung.
The sheriff found him hunched by a fire
fumbling to spit ram rib on willow limb.

His every effort hopeless
as the sprint he made toward Scout Mountain.
At dusk he gulped a prayer and clenched his eyes.

4.
We leave the shade and what flames out
has nothing to do with humankind.
No shining from meetinghouse steeple or bell.
Mouse nest, grouse turd, castoff
antler gnawed. These bits
of necessity lavished by dry light
afford reverence enough to keep speech plain.

Let them all go barefoot, rub dust in scalps
to gratify the dead. They've drunk
these waters before and come back whole.

MOLL GONE

I hooked men and I hooked lace.
Twin trades. After years
of labor I married but my mate
went bankrupt and died.
All his debts became mine to deny.

Past childbearing, money as gone
as my looks, fingers stiff
that once knitted lace on linen, I fell
afoul of an old client, a sharp,
a magistrate who forced me to choose:

I could beggar off to America or spend
my life in Marshalsea.
Join the syphilitics and the daft,
the buggerers and thieves.
I shipped for Boston that same week.

Now sermons from the pulpit pound
fierce or ponderous
as the text proceeds. The hourglass
turns and fills and
turns again. Dust motes crowd

light streaming down the sky.
Arthritic, I had hoped
to discover oversea a cure
in drier weather, purer drink.
Devotion makes my cartilage ache.

My joints need healing not my soul.
A poor dream calls me to rise
from my pew and kneel beside the sea.

Peace stands before me like a man.
He promises I might fling away my cane.

Instead I twist on my thin cot
stiff beyond all capacity to cry out.

Upcountry, I'm told, springs
bubble, surpassing wine for taste,
and a searching warmth endows the air.

THE GLARE OF HER AWARENESS

for Anne Hutchinson

Increase Mather demanded
how I knew I was hearing the Spirit.
The courtroom murmurs rose to a buzz.
Sweet as can be I asked him back,
How did Abraham know it was God
who asked him to offer Isaac?

Better to lead my friends in prayer
than to hear rebukes
from those who find my wit
fit only for reciting nursery rhymes.
No man of the cloth will ever
again disorder my sense of heaven.

Before they rode me off to jail
I kneaded wheat bread on my porch
and watched bees fumble
among the honeysuckle. The flour I puffed
from the breadboard settled
lightly on the leaves.

In the midst of the trial I learned
they want to see my child.
She lies in bits beneath the booted dirt.
Stir up her remnants, I won't mind.
She might rise like dragon teeth
and seek my detractors where they sleep.

THE BANQUET OF ST. ANTHONY

Townsfolk feature me a leech, as if health depends
on bugs that drink sick blood. But I slice
no veins or drain them to cups.
My craft turns on the simple leaves
unnoticed underfoot. Herbs alone can salvage

ebbing health. Mathias de L'Obel told my story
wrong. He said the monks
themselves brewed cordial cups
to ignite the fire. Not so! My hands
plucked the plants and crumbled them to dust.

Jesuits in black robes drifting down to Maine
hushed the tongues of Massachusetts
church bells. The Boston saints
desperate to rout the French
set to fretting Heaven nightly for a sign.

I distilled a plan. Knowing how French monks
like to render bread and wine into
a mocking type of Christ, I surmised how
soft and weak the flesh is in them.
I divined a sly cook might brew discord

between them and the townsfolk of St. Anthony,
the village that lay on Nova Scotia's shore
where the only mutual meat is fish
and the only drink a stout ale.
Under a captain's cloak I feigned shipwreck.

On shore I spoke their Popish tongue
and offered my ship's rescued mess as thanks
for respite from the storm. Then I claimed

a fever and said the restoration
of my ship would warrant a feast. Five nights

I watched what pride the order shadowed forth
in piety, in plain-song, coarse cloth
and celibacy. For five long days I read

the signature of their characters
and matched it to the doctrine of my lore.

Eryngo, damiana and satyrion root I found
the herbs best to unmask them.
Before the Earth I tendered my resolve
and it declared me fitting in a dream
where a vine-wreathed crucifix

lurched into consuming flame. The sixth day
I fetched my mess and fell to cooking
sauces, cakes, creams. My hosts
readied the banquet board. Ale flowed.
Into it I scattered all my dust and smiled

to see it sopped up. Next came a soup
of leeks and cheese, then tender partridge breasts
plump with stuffing and seasoned sound.
Chops of venison sighed smoke
from earthen trenchers. Merriment at table

grew when cakes and cordials came around.
Old wines broke bonds and splashed
to cups I'd lathered thick for the occasion.
Soon a quiet uproar filled the hall.
Soon a dozen monks spilled to the street

and called out the townsfolk. My herbs
had stirred in them a feral spirit
that needed swift outlet.
Their hunger focused first on the inn.
Peals of wild delight spiraled

to crashes and cries muffled by chamber walls
and the inhuman groan of appetites
long fenced by creed. What hour the chaos
ended I cannot say. Dawn found me
coasting south on fairer seas than I have ever

met with to this day. God's eye was rising
across the harbor when I fried
fresh-caught flounder to fracture my fast.
Thrushes in the riggings preened
and golden flowers washed in our wake.

WHEN LAND GROWS FAT

"A thousand Edens lost, and autumn
In the garden of old men
Is fall, is aimless, is a parade of pain."

—Patricia Goedicke

KIT GARDINER, BANISHED

Because I cared for Mistress Wheelwright too much
and dared not bind myself in wedlock knot
I am set adrift upon this frozen wild
though favored by fate to escape the scaffold rope.

Maybe some prowling freeman sent up word,
little pitchers have the busiest ears,
maybe the deputy heard our joyous cries.
I intone my woe that others might avoid my luck.

New England was to me a virgin land
where men unwracked by too much rent
might raise up cattle and crops. We invested
shrubs with new denominations, we pruned out
spindly shoots and grafted fruit to fruit.

What I did I did as any man might do
when land grows fat and saxifrages blow
among the rocky clefts. I plucked
a spray and proffered them at her door.
She admitted me. How was I to know her
father presided minister at Hampton Church?

We loved each other till our loving laughter
fell on the congregation's ears.
Then jealous hearts and bitter tongues
let merchant saints know that in their midst
an intruder was night-plowing
and humming obsessive musical deeds.

One afternoon I chanced to spy a hanging fruit.
It looked like a pineapple plated with scales.
This New World offers such treasures by the score.
But when I reached on toes to pluck it

a vapor of wasps swathed me
and stung till I knew not who I was.

If those same magistrates who drove me out of town
were to admit their own whims and urgings
they would be beside me now, starving
and hard-bitten by frost, for does the Bible not
enjoin us to root out sinful thoughts as well as deeds?

Whoever I am, I am as my creator made me.
There's a bit of prudence for you, as John Rhodes
liked to say. Look out for another home,
poor creature, one where men are less precise.

BUCK MEADOWS

A cinch strap tightening snug
once hemmed our breath.
Something so imperative and close
it bellowed mountain air
from nose, lips, lungs, blood.
Cantering heartbeat,
whistle between teeth, a thrum
as though from hooves
tattooed our pulses awake and swelled
the veins. Warblers flocked
north and one perched
skull-top, cocked above the rock.

Now, you murmured, and the dream
we had been rehearsing
slid wholly to light and slicked
the mountains gold.
Tooth chatter, finger croon,
prattle of lost tongues.
The pace of dawn-light quickened
frost to droplets.
Gold drenched our meadow bed
until the vision steadied
and we joined
the great stone of earth in its spin.

BENEDICTION

    For my straying wife

Within whatever woman affections rise
in May—blankets and wine
on a riverbank, poplars
swaying in sun-glare—
so that in secret she leans back on wool
no husband's hand may stop her
but she will
gravitate toward joy.
Cotton slipping in thin folds
down shinbones hitches at the heels.

Her tumbled hair floats free of the face
in a spray across grass.
Growth of river meadows,
sedge leaves, its sharp blades bend
to pierce the garland of hair.
Crowned that way she may
close both eyes and dream of grace
and how it turns to dust—
tender, scentless, cloud-soft.
Earth-sigh, too, she says, is heavened.

Protect her from courts and lawmen,
from angry reckonings
at midnight. Spare her home
from sickly curses
that rend the fabric of the air.
Free her brazen self
to plunge and fumble and plunge again.
As bay winds blown
to a schooner bring speed,
grant these new affections weather.

ANNIVERSARY

Streaked by gull dross,
the ramshackle beach shed,
its rooftop clacking
and yard thistle-grown.

But come in. The scrubbed threshold
bears up well.

Twelve years past,
my dear, you carried me
to this same goose-down mattress,
made believe you were my singing-master
and flung wide these sashes
to the sea. Many discursive feet
have not scoured dull
what gleams here.

Now the roof planks bang above us
beaming. Thistles nod.
Laughter is a bright canzone, sweetness,
the liquid melody
that gathers, clusters, refuses to fall.

MAGISTRATE

1.
From the steerhide couch in my chamber
I oversee the musing pace
of this town I founded in 1654.
I can scent the salt flats
wafting off the Massachusetts Bay.
Pleasures vexed by the groans
of James Corey being stone-pressed to confess.

I wanted to snap him by his smock
and shake his teeth. I wanted to say
Own up to your crimes and travel free.
Begin with your complicity in
bewitching Rachel Newman's milk cow.

2.
No beer at dinner for me this noon,
I tell my servant Marianne.
She's braided her hair in fetching reins
and loosed her bodice stays.
That girl would help bury my wife
if she were free to say so.

The law sometimes would devour me,
as today, would blunt the tip
of my goose quill pen.

Last month's case of Bishop Prate
discovered down in Maine
remains to be resolved
before week's end. Let him brood
upon his crime in the stocks another day.

A soldier from King Philip's War
seeks restitution
for his leg. He shall receive
an inspectorship on the Saybrook quay.

3.
The imported quince tree
outside my door
stirs in a noontide breeze.
Steam from lamb chops
on platter, lemon
white sauce, strong black tea
and maple cane.
Tell those men to stop
until I finish dining!

MARIANNE'S QUARTERS

The Father's floggings stung
less than his tongue. He swung
till my young will to love fell numb.

By the time I was fourteen
I knew no man should please me.
I smudged lard between my thighs
and helped the pup's nose
find it. My hand like a spider crept
down the belly spout.

Underneath men I could clench and let go
before breath whistled in my teeth
and they heard surrender.
Wind shivered the elm leaves but not me.

On a block in London he bought my time,
this second somber master,
and I became his
bonded five-year servant.
He spoke precisely, smelled of ham
and asked me to thank him
in his chamber on hands and knees.

He is magistrate in this New England town.
He has more power than the law allows.

In my quarters the chimney flue won't draw.
Green pitch pine wood smoke
causes me to wheeze. At his sideboard
I pour his beer, dish up meals,
two years and I'll be free.

The loaves of bread I baked
are steaming
and the butter is chilling on ice.

GRAIN ON THE FIELDS

1.
Hold me up a looking glass
to see my blotchy face;
sniff the rancid rye we milled
to bake a blackbird pie.
A fuzz of fungus sprouted
atop the flour in the community bin.
Sarah sifted it all the same
and latticed a crust.
We ate. Tongues and teeth
cleaved breast-flesh
from the cartilage and bone
as one might pit a plum. An hour later
we yawned, vomited, wept
at imps in the rafters hissing
and winging to pinch us where we lay.

2.
Oh succor, make it leave me be.
The fire-wheel
whose sparks fizz and scorch
now pintos the dark.
Hot needles gather and jab
within my corset stays.
Downwind of old cucumbers
rotting I wail and quake,
try to stride the sloping floor
until dull implosions
underneath the footboards
bring the watchtower sentry running.
At the last I palsy, topple,
wonder whose blood
is leaking from my swollen tongue.

3.
The head-high valley grasses
must have been
more living than these fields
fuzzed green with grain.
Our ancestors, tender-eyed,
compared the sight
of grasslands
to the sky, to the sea,
and to the blowing fur of beasts
in the beginning.
Larks, partridges, fowls of all sorts
bred and nested on the sod
and plow was a sound
seed heads made
when air went splashing past them.

MALAD

In middle spring of every year
the mountains due north
rumble. I felt the roar
last week when I went out
to feed the dogs.
Kip cowered by my legs.
It sounded as though a growl
were rising deep in the clogged throat
of some underground beast
and needing to burst
to find relief.
Or as though granite were to rasp
against flint to spark
and shoot up snowfield fires.
The rumbling pierced
my boot-soles, stung my scalp.
I was astride that beast
and the stones were grating me.

Do not think me someone whom
the brutal winters daze
and he begins to witness angels spinning
in trees, or hears harbor seals
barking Vulgate verse.
Fall and winter I cast lines and nets.
I split cod, dry the halves
on stages, salt and pack them into kegs.
In spring, though, I turn farmer.
I wake to sow the fields
and hope my timing's right.

How deep the tunneling roots
of rust pine and white oak
must plunge to rouse

the planet's crust. How far
the occasional cry of the raven stabs.
No longer do I take the rumble
as simple symptom of a crippled prince
risen to renew us. Now I hear
those Earth-tremors as
an antic devotion. As notice that
it's time to soften soil,
turn up worms, fling seeds.

From the doorway I send trial rings
of words the dogs echo.
The season's liquefying wind
breathes in and out of me.
I push the planet, I ask aloud
if winter's truly busted.
The rumbling mountains answer
yes, sow seeds now, green is trickling in.

MERCHANT SAINTS

"A set of people living on a frozen lake, surrounded by cliffs over which there is no escape, yet knowing that little by little the ice is melting, and the inevitable day drawing near when the last film of it will disappear, and to be drowned ignominiously will be the human creature's portion."

—William James

JOHN WINTER TO MOSES GOODYEAR

June ye 16th, 1642

Today a ship lowered anker in our island's wind shadow & sent a sailor down the fomeing breakers. After landing his skiffe the man stood off away from our fish-stages to hale us. Bless the weather, cried he. Have ye any sweating medicine laid up? None, we shouted & asked who he might be. Said he spoke for the *New Supply*, blown fresh from England but striken sore now with smallpox throughout the crew. After he made that revelation, we asked him to depart our shore & put our health at risk no more.

Ten days on the bay his crew spent in quarantine. We watched their boat wallow. Then back they sent Sir Thomas Rampling, an ancyent knight of four score years or more. His mates had sickend of the pox during passage, he explained; many lay moaning long in hammocks & some died. We told him to stand farther away. He bent over to show how they rendered unto Poseidon the contagious carcasses, by tying cannon balls about the necks of the dead & tossing them overboard. We flung him a cedar bundle wherewith to fume his cloathes & along with it a pipelode of our dearest smoke.

I write now to alert you that this man from his remarkes appears to be a dire opponent to the reformation at hand. He spoke of Calvin's "errours" & seemed to esteem the Book of Common Prayer. He intends to settle near Gorgeana. Your kind advice in this matter will be awaited. As evver, I am yours in loving servitude & faith.

COTTON MATHER, EXORCIST

To quell Henry's captive soul
I read Isaiah, fed him
tea brewed of valerian root,
and loosened the sheet
he clenched. An andiron reared
amid the coals of the hearth
and the sudden figure of a cat.

The animal sprung across the quilt
and clung to Henry's neck.
I sat petrified. He gasped,
thrashed, and abandoned all sense
till a holy curse split his lips
and everything fell still. The room stunk
of boiling tar. I doused the flames.

Still today, in my study or on the sea
that beast's nails shrewdly cleave
and I fall faint, my heart
faltering. I doubt whether Peter
when his mockers cursed him suffered
more than I from Henry's prayer.
Everyday his eyes possess me.

THE GREAT SWAMP FIGHT
FROM THE PULPIT CONSTRUED

Our new Israel has lain fallow till now,
unharrowed by wrath's keen blade,
allowing natives to stray our margins
and menace us. But in the Book of Leviticus
we find a promise: "I shall bring a Sword
that shall avenge the quarrel of the Covenant."

We learn there how to read King Philip's War:
as a judgment on the backsliding
so prevalent among us. These latter days
have given rise to unregenerate ways.
Far from our elder-wisdom we slip each week
and provoke the fury of our Father who sees fit

to cast us into battle. King Philip prayed in his way
for death to his English opponents,
prayed to Satan whom he called Abbamocho
deep in forest shades, prayed for his men
to deliver the scalp that Captain Church still wears.
How do we merit such sweet salve?

The savages exalt the wilderness and wine.
Their recklessness opens all six seals
to unspeakable lusts. Like restless thoughts
that haunt at the edge of sleep
they strive to bear away pure virgins
to the swamp where Philip's last act passed

and the mire wheezed and reeked of dreams.
There God suffered us there to slay
the barbarians—children, women and braves,
their blood meant to purge the earth

of all its corruptions. As pitiful as their cries
among the flames, scriptures declared them good.

We are the avenging sword of Leviticus today.
Let us turn it on heresy as we've always done—
Quaker, Shaker, Ranter and Antinomian.
Let us flourish dread above the heads
of every heathen creed. In the great swamp fight
King Philip fell. He regenerates us in his pretty death.

THE HAWTHORN TREE

Hunches on a bluff at Kennebec Bay
and strews the rocky beach
with haws—fleshy, red and rank.
From its mute fruits
our make and making sway.

A pair of doves bred in its thatch
till Morrell's boy's stone
overset the nest. The spilt yolks
left gashes on the beach.
The red hound bayed and chased

a raccoon to the thorny boughs.
William lit a mullein torch and shot it.
The animal dropped, a fur purse,
and lodged in a crotch.
Six months its ringtail dangled down.

Our colony grew. The oak woods fell
to yield grazing land or planks or staves.
Yet no one hazarded an ax to chop
the hawthorn. No one dared
to cut apart what nature heaved up.

One day a rusty cormorant claimed
the tree. It stretched, croaked,
gulped and spread wings
to soak up sun. An old-world token,
we agreed, and ran to scare it back to sea.

Doubt crowns this fractious land.
A strong hand will forever
daub the dying leaves with flame.

Long may the hawthorn's gift of tongues
ignite each berry it utters.

BARNYARD ARTIST

Dusk, the hour propels my blood
across the rutting cornfields.
Storm blasts shudder the mud-chinked
barn door frame I darken.
A handsome court clerk, out of reach,
frock coat billowing black
to buoy me back atop the world
but unsustaining, too late,
the howling wilderness of dream
already knuckling my knees.

The governor's young maid is bathing.
My fever forges the scene.
The oak-fed kettle's steam clouds
corners of the horn pane
and her master is gone to Malden
tonight. The business
my vigilance inscribes and seals
has a bylaw of its own—
corpus sanctum, repealing
the chill writs of *noli me tangere*.

The governor's young maid is gleaming,
the pine oil lamp light creeps
along her swung breasts tangibly,
she extends an ivory arm
to fasten back her unfurled hair.

From the barnyard high
as the peaked roof's weather cock
I am rising—eyes, groin,
each sweltering cell of soul aflame
and bleating with sheep,
bawling with goats and calves.

I pray my gratitude that
women, poor forked creatures,
be needy of the salve
my potion alone can furnish.

Animals too, the world's body,
brood to be soothed, taken by force.
They subpoena me to mount
the fragrant corncrib splintered
by beasts hungering salt.
Wool, dung, dander and lanolin
summon me and I join in
the universal keening toward conjunction.

BROOD SLAVE

    for the one bred

    Visitor to the Plantation

She crept out to me late one night
weeping. Said she'd been forced
to couple with a buck
she barely knew,
her first, bidden to come
to her bed.
          My host, I said,
desired to gain a breed of slaves.
She must submit to his will
because the Curse of Ham
lay upon her. This news she took
with disdain beyond grief.

    Master Maverick

I stood there in the shack
when the breeding took place
and I can testify
no damage came to Aphrodite.
I would never allow it, she's worth
four hundred dollars.
          Stand up
for a slattern wench?
Why, the way she raised howl
when I went to brand her ham
you'd have thought she was
Queen of Bathsheba herself.

Aphrodite

I can't say plain who I am
but I know well enough who I was.
My mother's throne would now be mine
but she died when I was twelve fighting men
who caught and bound and brought
      me here.
How can I tell it
so you will know? To be mounted
and have your master stare, to birth up
babes and suckle them on pain.
To love, to love…who? I will frock
my belly, hat my head, no man may see.

ARROWHEAD HUNTING AT KINPORT PEAK

The sun needled down on ancient bones,
on breasts and belly bare as my own
but darker. On your skin, fit
for towering heights like these, skin
burnished by ancestral grief
and heat. You wanted to guide me
up canyon and shale slide to say:
Here hunters waited for their prey.

Our hands sifted sand. Deer drifted
in pairs to the mineral lick,
their rough tongues trenching hollows.
We tried tasting the wall of salt.
Tasted ourselves and the sweet
beads of our inland seas;
it turned our crouching upside down.
Easy, laughing, seasoned sound,

we crushed weeds and furrowed dirt
searching for flint bits hurled
at deer, fallen from skin pouches,
dropped from slight wounds.
Flecks of mica sparkled your hair.
Cliffs swayed, I swear,
when at last we fell on the trail
winded and still twitching from the chase.

THE GREAT AWAKENING

Today in meeting Mr. Edwards said
we should all tumble into Hell
if God were to withdraw the web
that suspends us. How well
the spinner must have spun, how full of dread

we passed before the judgment bench to pay
due tribute. Chokes and sobs and vows
rose from the somber congregation.
He laid hand on a babe's brow
who slumbered through the sermon. "Nor will they

be spared, the innocents, our heavy blame
having stained them." So he invoked
our sins in tones low as though he prayed.
At last the newborn babe woke
whose mother shushed her and shone red in shame.

EPITAPH

Beneath the root-locked sod I ride
twin coppers pressing shut my eyes
and hair and fingernails grow wild

as morning glory. Come to prune
the tendrils, pluck the vetch, a fool
might think the effigy too crude

I carved upon this stone. I'll shake
alive his fear of Catholic ways.
He will likely tell the magistrate

that in the congregation's midst
worship the heirs of one who
built a granite icon. See the eyelids,

clamped shut a thousand years, flare
wide to behold the trumpet blast
with bodily eyes. Observe how shafts

of light transfix the sky. I wrought
these images to wrench the law
from ham-tongued preachers and their thralls

that people our courts. I can read
the scriptures well enough, can plead
my case although my lips be sealed.

Iconoclasts, this clumsy stone
will shatter idols all alone
if left intact above my bones.

NOTES

"Brooding Season" (page 1)
The section epigraph here is from John Berryman, *Homage to Mistress Bradstreet* (New York: Farrar, Straus and Giroux, 1956). Berryman dedicated that book-length poem to Anne Bradstreet (1612-1672), the first writer in England's North American colonies to be published.

"The Gorgeana Escorts" (page 5)
The town of York in Maine was first named Gorgeana after Sir Ferdinando Gorges, the Englishman who established the Province of Maine in 1622. Gorges was "an adventurer," a venture capitalist who never laid eyes on American soil but invested in it from afar.

"Michael Mitton" (page 6)
Like the other sections of "The Gorgeana Escorts," this is a loose American sonnet. It alludes to John Gerard's 1597 *Herball, or Generall History of Plantes*, the most popular book of botany in England in the 17th century.

"Song of Salmon" (page 8)
In 1931, anthropologist Franz Boas (1858-1942) extensively studied the Kwakiutl people, a name he used for the twenty-eight related tribes in coastal British Columbia. With the help of literate local ethnographers, he recorded the people's legends and songs. I translated this song from Boas' records.

"King Philip" (page 9)
A Wampanoag chief and warrior, known as Metacom or Metacomet (1638-1676), Philip was the second son of Massasoit. His tribe buried warriors in upright positions. Philip died in Rhode Island during the war named for him. Following his death, his wife and nine-year-old son were sold into slavery in Bermuda. The soldier who killed him received his right hand as a prize. For a quarter-century, Philip's head was displayed at Fort Plymouth, Massachusetts.

"How the Powwow Found Her" (page 10)
A powwow, the speaker of this poem, was a priest or shaman among North American Indians. The word preceded "shaman" in the English language.

"Thomas Morton" (page 11)
Author, lawyer, and social activist Morton (1579-1647) founded the colony of Merry Mount in the 1620s in what is now Quincy, Massachusetts. He ran afoul of Puritan authorities for fraternizing with Indians, trading liquor, and practicing "heathenism" by erecting a maypole and hosting dances. Those authorities, including Myles Standish and John Endecott, feared Morton's influence and suspected he had gone native. For his offenses, he was imprisoned several times, sickened by his imprisonment, and banished from the colony. In England in 1637, he published a three-volume satirical memoir and study of Native American culture titled *The New English Canaan*.

"Famacides" (page 13)
A famacide is a defamer or slanderer. The word survives in legal discourse today. The speaker of this poem is an imagined grandchild of Thomas Morton, that rebel lawyer in the colonies.

Section epigraph (page 19)
From "Testimonial," in *On the Bus with Rosa Parks*, by Rita Dove. New York: Norton, 1999. Born in 1952, Dove won the Pulitzer Prize for Poetry in 1987 for her monologue cycle *Thomas and Beulah* (Carnegie Mellon, 1986).

"Sarah Hawkridge" (page 20)
In some accounts named Sarah Hawkredd (1600-1676), she wed the Reverend John Cotton in 1632, a leading clergyman and teacher in the Massachusetts Bay Colony. None of the poems she is alleged to have written survived the historical record, although many of her husband's poems have.

"Here and Now" (page 25)
Epigraph from Emile Jean-Baptist Marie Grouard, *Beginning of Print Culture in Athabasca Country*. Edmonton: University of Alberta Press, 2012.

"Governor Winthrop" (page 28)
John Winthrop (1587-1649) was chosen governor of the Massachusetts Bay Colony several times between 1631 and 1648. He led prosecutions against both Mary Dyer (1611-1660) and Anne Hutchinson for heresies. Dyer bore a deformed and stillborn baby on October 11, 1637. Before a large crowd the next year, Winthrop had the child's corpse exhumed as part of the legal proceedings. After trying and convicting Hutchinson, he banished her.

Section epigraph (page 31)
From the 1642 history *Of Plymouth Plantation* by the English Separatist leader William Bradford (c. 1590-1657), who governed the Plymouth Colony in Massachusetts for more than thirty years. The quoted passage comments on the alleged behavior of Thomas Granger, the speaker of "Barnyard Artist."

"Tenochtitlan" (page 32)
Tenochtitlan, a city-state founded in 1325 on an island on Lake Texcoco, housed the palace of Montezuma II and served as capital of the Aztec Empire. Montezuma's palace in Tenochtitlan had two zoos, several aviaries, an aquarium, and a botanical garden that furnished occupations for three hundred attendants. Hernando Cortés conquered the people in 1521. Some say he wholly broke their spirits by setting fire to the largest of their aviaries.

"Ouzel" (page 35)
Ouzel is the European name for a semi-aquatic bird that nests behind waterfalls and makes its living within streams. The variant species on the North American continent is known as the American dipper (*Cinclus mexicanus*). It has a second eyelid, called a nictitating membrane, that

allows it to see underwater. The epigraph is from *Macbeth* by William Shakespeare.

"Crossing Arbon Valley" (page 38)
Part of the Fort Hall Indian Reservation in southeastern Idaho, Arbon Valley was colonized and is populated today predominantly by the Mormon faithful, aka the Latter-Day Saints.

"The Glare of Her Awareness" (page 42)
Anne Hutchinson (1591-1643) was a lay religious leader who rebelled against the leaders of the Massachusetts Bay Colony. She immigrated there in 1634 and began leading prayer sessions in her home, emphasizing individual relationships with deity instead of relying on ministers to mediate. Governor John Winthrop and others viewed her practices as blasphemy. In 1637, while she was pregnant, they took her to court and charged her with eighty-eight "errours." After being excommunicated and banished, she bore a stillborn child and was murdered by Siwanoy people in New Netherland. Her foes took the birth and murder as substantiation of divine judgment against her.

"The Banquet of St. Anthony" (page 43)
Matthias de L'Obel (1538-1616) was a Flemish physician and botanist for James I of England and other rulers in Europe. He published his *Images of Plants, both Exotic and Native* in 1591. An account in L'Obel's book furnishes the narrative seedbed for this poem.

Section epigraph (page 47)
Patricia Goedicke (1931-2006) was an American poet who studied with Robert Frost.

"Grain on the Fields" (page 57)
One possible cause of the 1692 Salem Witchcraft Trials was tainted grain. Convulsive ergotism results from ergot fungus (*Claviceps purpurea*). It grows on rye and its effects may have been mistaken for demonic possession. Victims display symptoms that correspond with court records

of the events in Salem, where twenty people were executed, mostly by hanging. Symptoms include vertigo, tinnitus, convulsions, muscular contractions, melancholy, hallucinations, delirium, vomiting and diarrhea. The colony later admitted the trials were a mistake and made reparations to the families of the convicted.

Section epigraph (page 61)
From William James, *The Varieties of Religious Experience: A Study in Human Nature* (1902). In this passage James was commenting on the psychological condition of those he termed the "sick souls" of religious fundamentalism.

"Cotton Mather, Exorcist" (page 63)
Mather (1663-1728) was a minister, an author of sermons and pamphlets, a Fellow of the Royal Society, and an expert witness in the Salem Witchcraft Trials. His use of "spectral evidence" in those trials accorded him his credibility. He studied Salem residents whom he believed to be possessed, and he made efforts as a minister to deliver them from seeming evil.

"The Great Swamp Fight from the Pulpit Construed" (page 64)
In King Philip's War (1675-76), the battle that toppled the Wampanoag leader Metacom or King Philip is known as the Great Swamp Fight.

"Barnyard Artist" (page 68)
Governor William Bradford of Plymouth Plantation reported in 1642 that citizen Thomas Granger "was this year detected of buggery, and indicted for the same, with a mare, a cow, two goats, five sheep, two calves and a turkey." His punishment took the following form: "first the mare and then the cow and the rest of the lesser cattle [i.e., animals] were killed before his face, according to the law, Leviticus XX.15, and then he himself was executed."

"Barnyard Artist" (page 68)
Fleshes out Granger's backstory as a copyist or legal scribe, whose confessional here is laden with the language of the law. The phrase

"horn pane" references the material that common people used to make windows. Cattle horns soaked for months in water were split, flattened, and fashioned into kinds of panes to let in light. *Corpus sanctum*: holy body. *Noli me tangere*: touch me not.

"Brood Slave" (page 70)
Like brood hens and brood mares (animals kept expressly for producing offspring or eggs), female slaves were used to produce marketable children. The biblical Curse of Ham, imposed by Noah upon one of his sons, was interpreted by some believers to offer both an explanation for black skin and a justification for slavery. See Genesis 9: 20-27.

"The Great Awakening" (page 73)
The Puritan divine Jonathan Edwards (1703-58), in 1741 at the height of the New England religious revival known as the first Great Awakening, preached his renowned sermon "Sinners in the Hands of an Angry God." The sermon combines horrific images of Hell with warnings against backsliding or relapsing. The sermon so terrified his congregation, according to reports, that listeners interrupted him with moans and cries and pleas for their salvation.

"Epitaph" (page 74)
Gravestone iconography told stories that were mostly doctrinaire and dogmatic. One topic, the Apocalypse, depicted Christ's return to separate the unregenerate from those who were destined to be saved. The speaker of this poem carved his own gravestone. In doing so he took the risk that iconoclasts—literally, "icon smashers"—would find his images sinful for perceived idolatry and smash the headstone with cudgels and clubs. Puritans were suspicious of depicting humans because Catholics had often done so.

ABOUT THE AUTHOR

Paul Lindholdt is a professor of English at Eastern Washington University, with a PhD in early American literature. His preparation in poetry began with a graduate degree when he studied with Annie Dillard and won an Academy of American Poets Prize. Shortly thereafter he began publishing these poems in *Beloit Poetry Journal*, *Chicago Review*, *Poet Lore*, *Poetry Northwest*, *Sewanee Review*, and *Southern Humanities Review*. All told, twenty-four of these forty-five poems have appeared in arts journals, history journals, and standalone books.

www.ingramcontent.com/pod-product-compliance
Lightning Source LLC
Chambersburg PA
CBHW030158100526
44592CB00009B/347